Girl, Be Free
How to Recover from Trauma and Embrace Femininity

Daye'Jai Golston

Girl, Be Free: How to Recover from Trauma and Embrace Femininity

Copyright © 2022 Daye'Jai Golston

All rights reserved. No part of this book may be reproduced or used in any manner without the prior written permission of the author, except for the use of brief quotations in a book review.

Unless otherwise stated, all Scripture is taken from the New King James Version®. Copyright © 1982 by Thomas Nelson. Used by permission. All rights reserved.

Also used: New Living Translation, copyright © 1996, 2004, 2015 by Tyndale House Foundation. Used by permission of Tyndale House Publishers, Inc., Carol Stream, Illinois 60188. All rights reserved.

This book is dedicated to the beautiful Pastor Sha'Da Taylor! Your elegance and flow sowed seeds of healing and femininity in me. I pray that as you read the pages ahead, you'll be encouraged to know that your labor is never in vain!

CONTENTS

Introduction	Pg #1
Chapter 1: What is Femininity? Physical, Mental & Emotional Components of the Feminine Woman	Pg #5
Chapter 2: Blindsided by Trauma: The Disempowered Woman	Pg #15
Chapter 3: It's Okay to Be Free: Beginning the Journey of Healing	Pg #29
Chapter 4: Life Through the Lens of a Feminine Woman: Proverbs 31 Study	Pg #43
Chapter 5: The Power of Vulnerability: Forgiveness Within the Healing Process	Pg #67
Chapter 6: It's Okay to be Free Part II: Practical Ways to Embrace Femininity	Pg #81
Chapter 7: Boss Lady: Femininity and the CEO	Pg #95
Chapter 8: Mommy Hen: Femininity and the Single Mother	Pg #99
Chapter 9: Mrs. Right: Femininity and the Married Woman	Pg #107
Final Thought	Pg #113
About the Author	Pg #117

Introduction

"I want to finish the divorce," my then husband said. I sat there paralyzed. Disgust and regret permeated the living room. I walked over to the couch where my son was sitting. Holding back tears, I held him close attempting to rediscover any joy that might be left in my life. For months I fought off suicidal thoughts. My life was crumbling before my eyes—shattering into tiny pieces. I was unemployed, our house was on the verge of foreclosure, and I was driving a car in desperate need of repairs that I couldn't afford. *How did I get here? Am I to blame?*

I thought about the times I was told I was worthless and wouldn't amount to anything. I remembered the times I was called out of my name. I reflected on the moments I was painted as overly aggressive and too dominant. I thought about the people who were no longer in my life because of my foolish mistakes. *I have pure motives*, I thought to myself, *and yet I still push people away.*

It was at this moment that I had an epiphany. I wasn't necessarily a bad person. I just hadn't embraced my identity as the woman God created me to be. This was negatively impacting every area of life: my wellbeing, my children, and the people I attracted.

The trauma of rape, molestation, abuse and abandonment was holding me captive. I thought I had healed from it and moved on, but I was wrong. I had only become distant from my trauma. Throughout my childhood, I had to be my own protector and provider, so I didn't know how to embrace my womanhood and femininity. The many disappointments of my past led me to adopt a masculine core in an attempt to feel safe. I even lived a homosexual lifestyle. I vowed to never ask or receive help from anyone!

God met me in this moment of despair, and He invited me into a place of freedom. He took me on a journey of healing, and I finally discovered the woman I was born to be. And He wants to do the same for you. If you have experienced any traumatic situation in your life, this book is for you. If you are wounded and in desperate need of help, this book is for you. If you are struggling with your identity as a woman, this book is for you. As you read these pages and apply the principles in them, you will find healing from past traumas and finally walk in the freedom that comes with embracing your God-given identity as a woman. May your life never be the same in Jesus' name! Amen!

1

What is Femininity?

Physical, Mental & Emotional Components of the Feminine Woman

Have you ever been told you were too masculine? Too dominant or aggressive? Have you ever felt as if men were intimidated by you? I sure have. In fact, if I had a dollar for every time I was called aggressive, I would be on the verge of millionaire status! Interestingly enough, instead of being offended by this, I saw it as a badge of honor—I was proud of it. I knew God called me to be a businesswoman and a warrior for Him, so I thought it was natural for me to exude masculine energy. I even made statements like, "this is just who I am!" I had developed a masculine core as a result of the trauma I had experienced, and it was doing more harm than I had realized.

Men are blessed with God-given masculinity. To a certain degree, women embody some masculine characteristics, however, our natural core is feminine. Masculinity is marked by power, dominance, and control, and I was obsessed with all three. In my mind, the more intimidating I was, the better. I believed that the more I controlled a conversation, the more success I could gain. But baby, this was stressful! I lacked peace of mind. My relationships were strained, and I lost my sense of creativity and wonder. I could not see or enjoy the beauty of life because I was resisting instead of embracing femininity.

According to Webster's Dictionary, femininity is defined as "The quality or nature of the female sex: the quality, state, or degree of being feminine or womanly." When I originally read this definition at the beginning of my journey, I was offended and could feel my nostrils flaring in disgust. *Who in the world has the authority, let alone the audacity, to define womanhood for me? No! Women can be just as aggressive as men, and we can do everything a man can do. Sometimes better!*

This was my mentality. But after disappointment upon disappointment, I had to ask myself, am I thinking about this the right way? I took a step back and pondered why I was offended.

The truth is that I wanted to be feminine. I wanted to tap into those God-given characteristics, but I didn't know how. It was easier for me to declare with boldness that feminine traits weren't needed or necessary to be a woman, because it was my defense mechanism. I wasn't ready to face the truth, and the truth was that I didn't know how to embrace my femininity.

Before we go further, let me clarify a few things. First things first, I absolutely believe that women have the capacity and ability to do some of the same things as men. Secondly, femininity is less about *what* we do and more about *who* we are. Thus, femininity is the capacity and ability to embrace one's natural design as a woman. It can be broken down into three main categories: physical, mental, and emotional. This is the guide we will use to discuss some of the primary characteristics of the feminine woman. Let's get started!

A woman's physical body is naturally designed differently from men. Our bodies are created to nurture and sustain life. Genetically, both men and women possess estrogen and testosterone; however, women produce much more than men. [1] Of course, there are exceptions where the opposite is true, and, in those cases, doctors can prescribe medication to regulate the hormones back to proper balance. Estrogen is one of the reasons why women have more delicate features. It's because of estrogen that women have an increase in the accumulation of subcutaneous fat in our bodies. [2] That increase of fat creates a layer of padding directly under our skin, and it's why we are softer to touch than men. This softness brings comfort and warmth to the ones we love in a way that a man could never bring. Also, women are born with a reproductive system that gives us the ability to receive and create life. These organs include the womb, vagina, fallopian tubes, and ovaries. [3] Additionally, a woman's waist are generally more defined than men, and our hips are wider so that we can endure childbirth.

There is much beauty and variation when it comes to women's bodies. A woman's metabolism converts food to fat, and it stores that fat in our breasts, hips, and buttocks. [4] This makes our bodies curvier than (and more attractive to) the opposite sex. Contrary to what society may say, all body types are beautifully and wonderfully feminine. It's scientifically proven that women are generally shorter than men. However, I am considered tall, and I say with assurance that being tall or taller than some men does not mean you are any less feminine. It just means God made you tall. The roundness in a woman's face is also a major difference between women and men, although there are some women who God has blessed to have more structured facial features. No matter the variation, the feminine woman is connected and in tune with her body. She embraces the features God has given her, and she appreciates how different they are compared to that of a man.

Emotionally, the feminine woman is nurturing, caring and kind. She's soft and tender-hearted. She goes with the flow of life and remains calm and relaxed. The feminine woman is wise, and she relinquishes the need to control a situation, person, or outcome. She is a master of radical acceptance. She is patient and empathetic, vulnerable, and flexible. She knows how to adapt to her environment. She's giving and loyal, collaborative and connected. She lives in humility, and she is always open to receiving joyfully.

You see, the feminine woman provides everything that is needed for growth and development. We see this in mothers who nurture their children from birth to adulthood. We see this in teachers who go above and beyond to ensure the success of their students. Whether she's giving an encouraging word or cooking a nourishing meal, the feminine woman is present and in tune with those she nurtures. People feel safe to grow in her presence. With gentleness, the feminine woman sets an atmosphere that is conducive for expansion—she sees a need and wants to help in any way that she can. Not only is the feminine woman nurturing toward others, but she is also nurturing toward herself. She knows how to rest and care for herself mentally, physically, and emotionally, and she knows how to express what she needs with kindness.

Women who embrace their femininity exude gentleness. They are soft in action and mild-mannered. They speak with intentionality and politeness. The feminine woman knows how and when to back down. She is present and embraces her feelings. She flows with life one moment at a time and is flexible in her responses. Going back to genetics, women have a more developed limbic system than men, and the limbic system is responsible for regulating behavior, emotions, and memory. [5] The feminine woman can live in and express her emotions in a very healthy way.

Mentally, femininity involves being intuitive or knowing. For centuries women have been known for having a secret power of intuition. One of the reasons why a woman's intuitiveness is so powerful is because women have an innate ability to view things beyond logic. We know how to analyze scenarios, facial expressions, and body language. Oftentimes, we are more likely than men to follow certain mental impulses, and we are much more receptive to our inner thoughts.

The feminine woman is imaginative and creative. Her visualization skills are strong, and she can manifest in the physical realm what she has seen in her mind. If not used wisely, this can wreak havoc when a woman imagines a negative picture in her mind and acts on her impulses. Can you see how awesome and powerful women are? The feminine woman is a force to be reckoned with!

I mentioned earlier that femininity is about who you are, not what you do. You can be a basketball player, bodybuilder, or commercial truck driver and still embrace your femininity as a woman. Femininity is the essence of who one is as a woman. It's knowing you have been uniquely designed in your physical, mental, and emotional makeup to nurture, love and care for the people God has placed in your life. You can be a basketball player and still be nurturing and loving. You can be a bodybuilder and still exude gentleness. No matter what our career choice, it's important for us to understand that femininity is not one dimensional. We all have different passions and callings, and we can fulfill them while embracing our God-given identity as feminine women.

Take a moment to reflect on this chapter and identify where you are on the feminine spectrum. Some of you may embody many attributes of the feminine woman. On the other hand, some of these characteristics may be completely foreign to you. You may not see some of these attributes in your life right now and that is okay. No matter where you find yourself, I want you to know that you have been shaped and fashioned with amazing components. Don't receive the standards the world lives by when it comes to womanhood. You, Woman, have been designed by God, and we need you in this world! The fact that you're reading this book is evidence that you're ready to recover from trauma and thrive as the feminine woman you were born to be. So, take a deep breath, embrace where you are and reflect without condemnation. When you're ready, let's move forward and unpack trauma.

2

Blindsided by Trauma: The Disempowered Woman

I experienced a lot of traumas as a child. My mother was a teen parent, and she didn't have a healthy relationship with her mother. I would even venture to say that my grandmother didn't have a healthy relationship with her mother either. It seemed to be a generational cycle. Though my mother did the best she could, I grew up feeling abandoned. I remember living in the projects of Cleveland, babysitting my siblings and cousins while my mother and aunt enjoyed their youth. I cooked meals, helped with homework, and disciplined bad behavior. I tried to the best of my ability to be a mother while I was still just a kid.

From what I can remember, my father was incarcerated for the majority of my childhood. When I was fourteen, I found out he was not my biological father. Even though I acted like I was unbothered, it shattered me. I felt like an orphan. Not only did I feel a lack of connection to my mother, now I didn't know who my biological father was.

As a teenager, I felt like the black sheep of the family, and this made me angry. I bounced around from house to house and even lived with different members of the church I attended. The only person I felt safe around was my grandmother, and she was struggling with a crack addiction. As a child, I never knew this. It wasn't until the day my mother read an intervention letter out loud to my grandmother that I found out about her dependency. My grandmother later died from lung cancer, and, once again, I felt alone in this world. I had a need for validation and a longing to belong. Rejection crippled me. I sought love in all the wrong places, and this led to many dangerous situations and abusive relationships. I felt trapped. I knew I needed to leave, but I stayed because I thought it was what I deserved.

I even experienced trauma within my marriage. There were many times I felt unprotected and unsafe. I remember being eight months pregnant with swollen, aching ankles. Instead of being supported and encouraged to rest, I had to walk to get on the RTA route in the winter to make sure my kids got to school. There were physical altercations I experienced that no one knew about. I felt alone and suicidal, but I didn't feel safe enough with anyone to share what I was going through.

The effects of trauma continued to follow me and overshadowed every fiber of my being. Even as a believer, I self-sabotaged every friendship, relationship and opportunity that presented itself. What I didn't realize was that I hadn't fully healed. I had become a disempowered woman. Even though I received salvation and confessed to be a believer in Jesus Christ, I had yet to break free from the subconscious belief that I was nothing.

Trauma is lethal experiences that drastically change a person's life. It's something that may not appear lethal because some of us have survived and moved on with our lives. However, trauma *is* lethal from the standpoint that it can leave us disempowered and emotionally paralyzed. Trauma has the potential to affect us years after the initial experience, and it impacts our daily relationships and interactions with other people.

Francis Galton, a renowned psychologist, and inventor in the 1800s, had an interesting theory called nature vs. nurture. He concluded that human behavior is influenced more by our genetics (nature) than our environment and surroundings (nurture). [6] It is my belief, however, that in reference to femininity, a woman's ability to embrace her natural born feminine traits is largely influenced by the way she was raised. Sometimes we experience trauma and other life-changing events that cause us to shut down, and, as a result, we lose our interest in and/or ability to embrace our femininity.

Some of us were physically abused as children. We may have been raped or molested. I am a witness of how life-changing this type of trauma can be. It strips us of our innocence. We walk away from this experience never wanting anyone else to harm us that way again, so we shield ourselves to prevent people from seeing our vulnerability. Woman, you are not alone, and I invite you to be free!

Some of us have been verbally abused. We were made to feel like we weren't good enough. We were called unimaginable names, and we weren't given the affirmation needed to thrive in this life. We felt trapped and alone. Woman, you are not alone, and I invite you to be free!

Some of us have been emotionally abused. We were called overly emotional and dramatic, and we were made to feel as if our feelings weren't valid or important. We vowed that we would never allow anyone to make us feel this way again. We shut out the world and put up a facade that nothing affects us. Woman, you are not alone, and I invite you to be free!

Some of us have experienced abandonment from a parent, spouse, or loved one. We thought this person would be there for us in a particular time in our lives, but they weren't. It caused us to feel unsafe, inadequate, and unworthy of love. Woman, you are not alone, and I invite you to be free!

Some of us don't have great relationships with our fathers, and what's more, some of us may not even know our biological fathers! This form of trauma can cause us to feel unwanted. We may also feel unsafe and unprotected, so we vow to be our own protectors. Woman, you are not alone, and I invite you to be free!

Some of us faced difficult circumstances during childhood, so we had to grow up at a young age. Our mothers may have been sick or absent, and we had to care for younger siblings. This may have caused us to reject our femininity and take on a more dominant persona. Woman, you are not alone, and I invite you to be free!

For some of us, our childhood trauma expressed itself in insecurities and a lack of self-worth. We don't see our beauty, and when we look in the mirror, we feel worthless. Woman, you are not alone, and I invite you to be free!

Some of us may have been taken advantage of. People may have mistaken our kindness for weakness. Cheating, abuse, or manipulation in our romantic relationships have caused us to shut down completely. Woman, you are not alone, and I invite you to be free *today*!

The first step in freedom is determining whether or not you have healed *completely* from trauma. Sometimes the trauma is so deep-seated that we may think we've healed, but when we are blindsided—triggered by a conversation or situation—we see the long-term effects of trauma rear its ugly head.

When a driver has limited visibility, we call this a blind spot. Blind spots are areas on the sides of the car that can't be seen from the rearview or side mirrors. In fact, one must physically turn around to be sure those areas are clear. When a driver is blindsided, she is hit or attacked in the blind spot. Long-term effects of trauma live in our blind spots.

My blind spot came in the form of good deeds with wrong motives. Though I have always been a giver and found joy in my ability to give to others, my generosity was conditional. Whenever I felt my actions were unnoticed or unappreciated, I became resentful, angry, and bitter. I would exhaust myself—saying yes to everything—in an attempt to be worthy in the eyes of others, even God. I took on every task I possibly could to receive love and affirmation. I just wanted to be good enough. Though I had addressed the ways trauma had impacted my life, I hadn't confronted the effects hidden in my blind spot.

Oftentimes, we address and confront our trauma from the rear and side mirrors of our lives. We may go to therapy and seek wise counsel. We may write letters to the ones who hurt us to free ourselves from the pain they caused. We may read a self-help book and participate in different support groups. All these things are effectual, but it's possible to still have blind spots. So, how can we determine if we have fully healed from trauma? How can we uncover our blind spots?

Blind Spot Inventory: Characteristics of the Disempowered Woman

Read the following statements below that describe the disempowered woman. She is the opposite of the feminine woman described in chapter one. Check all the statements that are true about you.

In the last 6 months to a year...

- I have felt insecure or worthless.
- I have gossiped about another woman.

- I have been jealous of another woman.
- I have been prideful.
- I have felt like I'm better than someone else.
- I have told someone what they wanted to hear to gain their favor.
- I have tried to manipulate a person or situation.
- I have rejected help and tried to do everything on my own.
- I have pushed men away.
- I have relied on someone else's opinion of me to shape how I feel about myself.
- I have tried to control a person or situation.
- I have constantly apologized for things that were out of my control.
- I have felt powerless.
- I have felt overwhelmingly fearful.
- I have felt stressed.

Did you check off many boxes? Don't feel discouraged! There was a time when I checked off every box on this list. Remember the nature/nurture theory. We are not born with these emotions. They are a product of trauma. But freedom can be achieved when we know our blind spots and do the work of healing. Read on to learn more about the disempowered woman.

The disempowered woman is insecure and codependent. She doesn't have confidence in herself, and she doesn't see her self-worth. The thing about insecurity is that it can appear in the form of worthlessness but also in the form of pride and overconfidence. The disempowered woman who feels insecure can become codependent. Webster defines codependency as "a psychological condition or a relationship in which a person manifesting low self-esteem and a strong desire for approval has an unhealthy attachment to another often controlling or manipulative person." The disempowered woman is an enabler, and she may shield or protect an individual who abuses a substance or engages in other destructive behaviors. The codependent, disempowered woman has a need for approval and a fear of abandonment. She is extremely needy and has an unhealthy dependence on others' support, compliments, and applause.

The disempowered woman is dominating and controlling. She may feel superior over others, and she may or may not realize it. This woman craves control, and she has a fear of being helpless. She may have been hurt in the past and didn't have any control over her circumstances. Now, she tries to control the outcome of every situation. The disempowered woman avoids anything that makes her feel weak or gives the appearance of a lack of control.

The disempowered woman is manipulative. Women have the power to influence the environment around them, and the disempowered woman uses this superpower to manipulate others. She may forge documents, tell people what they want to hear, or "work her hand," as I like to say, so that she gets what she wants. It is her way or the highway! Period! I was once this woman!

The disempowered woman is jealous and envious of others, and she enjoys gossiping. Someone may have criticized and abused her in the past, and this trauma, although she may not admit it, has caused her to feel inadequate, unworthy, and powerless. As a result, she criticizes and puts people down—she murders the reputation of others with her words and actions. The disempowered woman can't resist highlighting the flaws in others, but she is unable to admit her own faults and shortcomings.

The disempowered woman lacks emotional self-control. She is overly apologetic, and it's very difficult for her to set boundaries. She is overwhelmed by her emotions, and she doesn't know how to express them in a healthy way. The disempowered woman has a fear of abandonment; therefore, she apologizes profusely to avoid conflict and rejection. She sacrifices healthy boundaries to receive (what she believes to be) love and affection.

The disempowered woman often feels stressed and trapped. She doesn't know how to balance her feminine and masculine energy, which we will discuss in chapter eight. She feels guilt and shame about her past mistakes and experiences. The disempowered woman is also naïve and conforming. It is difficult for her to leave a partner who is abusive and takes her for granted. She can also be conforming—" submitting to societal stereotypes and limiting herself to socially acceptable conventions or standards" (Oxford Dictionary).

The disempowered woman doesn't know how to build healthy relationships with men. She often feels intimidated by men and doesn't know how to flow in her femininity while interacting with a man. She pushes men away and has, what I call, the "independent black woman syndrome." She views men as unnecessary, and she rejects help because she wants to do everything on her own. She may have been let down before, and she vows to herself that she will never rely on another man again.

<div style="text-align:center">~~~</div>

Take another moment to breathe and reflect. Discussing these blind spots may feel like ripping a bandage off a wound. But in order to heal, a wound needs to be cleaned, given ointment and exposure to oxygen. By getting honest with yourself and identifying your blind spots, you're setting the stage for healing. Grab a sheet of paper and write down how you're feeling. What are your blind spots? What characteristics of the disempowered woman do you see in your own life? Keep this paper close to you—place it in this book if you need to—because in the next chapter, you will discover the practical steps to take to be free from trauma and walk in the newness of life!

3

It's Okay to Be Free: Beginning the Journey of Healing

Repeat after me: It's okay to be free!

It may seem like a simple concept, but sometimes we need to give ourselves verbal permission to break free of the habits and thought patterns that no longer serve us. Often, we live in the shame of our trauma and carry the guilt of poor choices, but freedom is possible! Freedom is available! Give yourself permission to be free.

After I became aware of my blind spots, I made the conscious decision to heal. Thus, I share with you that the journey of healing begins with a decision. It's one thing to *know* we need healing, but it's another thing to *apply* what we know so that healing can take place. Freedom isn't a feeling or an emotion, but rather a decision. Here are six strategies you can apply as you begin embracing your femininity.

1. *Retrain your thoughts & shift your perspective*

As previously mentioned, we fail to embrace our femininity because of our response to trauma. If you want to live a life of freedom, you must shift your perspective by retraining your thoughts. My favorite place to access new thoughts and perspectives is the Bible, because it is the only truth that will never fade away. It is "alive and powerful…sharper than the sharpest two-edged sword…" (Heb. 4:12 NLT). God's word cannot "return to [Him] void—it must accomplish what [He] pleases" (Isa. 55:11). Using the scriptures to retrain your thoughts is not only healthy, but it carries a powerful assurance.

This is what I do: I take any negative thought I have, then find a scripture in the Bible to counteract the negative thought. I use this scripture to form a new thought or perspective (see the chart on the next page for a list of 16 examples). I repeat the new thought (often out loud) along with the scripture it came from. I say it over and over until it becomes my reality. This is how you shift your perspective and ultimately change your life.

As you begin this process, it may seem as if nothing is happening at first. To be honest, the enemy may try to discourage you with even more negative thoughts. But be encouraged! Keep saying your new thoughts out loud with your referencing scriptures. Continue to make your new confessions! Write the scriptures on flashcards and start memorizing them (yes, you have some work to do), so you can write God's word "on the tablet of your heart" (Prov. 7:3). Use the scriptures as a weapon whenever your old thoughts try to return and take over.

I was serious about my healing to the point that I carried a small notepad with scriptures everywhere I went. Whenever a self-defeating thought would arise, I took out my notepad and reminded myself of the truth of God's word. I read my new thought and reference scripture out loud in its entirety. I did this so often that I started to memorize them. There is power in the Word of God, and it is indeed a weapon! Your background and qualifications don't matter when we speak the Word. When we receive Jesus as our

Lord and Savior (you can do this now if you haven't already), we become the recipient of every promise mentioned in the Bible! Speak and transform your new thoughts by faith knowing El Roi (the God who sees) sees and hears you. He *will* honor His Word.

Old Thoughts (Trauma-based)	**New Thoughts (Freedom-based)**
I am better than her/him.	I choose to be humble, because it is only by the mercies of God that I am where I am today. Lamentations 3:22 says "through the Lord's mercies that we are not consumed, because His compassions fail not!"
I am powerless.	I am "more than [a] conqueror through Him who loved [me]" according to Romans 8:37.
I don't have what I need.	According to Philippians 4:19, my God promised me "He will supply all [my] need according to His riches in glory by Christ Jesus."
I am inadequate.	I am created "in the image of God" according to Genesis 1:27, and I am more than enough!
I am unworthy.	God says I am worthy! I am "precious in [His] eyes…and honored and [He] has loved me" according to Isaiah 43:4.
God doesn't want	God is my "refuge and my strength," and

to help me.	He is *always* ready to "help" me in times of trouble according to Psalm 46:1.
I don't deserve financial security.	God "takes pleasure in [my] prosperity" according to Psalm 35:27, and He wishes "that [I] prosper in all things and be in health, just as [my] soul prospers" according to 3 John 1:2 (Yes honey! Don't be afraid to take full authority and use multiple scriptures to back up your new thoughts and confessions).
I can't do this!	Philippians 4:13 says "I can do *all things* through Christ who strengthens me," and this is what I believe!
Nothing good ever happens to me.	Jeremiah 29:11 says that "[God] knows the thoughts that [He] thinks toward [me]...thoughts of peace and not of evil, to give [me] a future and a hope," and this is what I believe!
I am unlovable, and nobody loves me.	God loves me so much that "He gave His *only begotten* Son" to die for me so that I can live a victorious life for all eternity with Him according to John 3:16.
My life has no value, and I see no point in living.	God has an amazing purpose for my life, and He knew me even before "I was formed in the womb" according to Jeremiah 1:5 (I encourage you to read this entire chapter and allow God to speak to you if this is a thought you struggle with).
God doesn't love me.	I am convinced that *nothing* "shall be able to separate [me] from the love of God..." according to Romans 8:38.
I am afraid.	God has not given [me] a spirit of fear, but

	of power and of love, and of a sound mind" according to 2 Timothy 1:7.
I deserve poor relationships.	I am worthy of and only accept healthy relationships that embody the love of Christ and the meaning of love according to 1 Corinthians 13.
I am a failure.	I believe "all things [are working] together for [my] good" according to Romans 8:28, and I choose to use the wisdom of my past to make better decisions for my future.
I have to manipulate this person or situation, or else things won't go well for me.	I choose to live in perfect love, and "perfect love casts out fear" according to 1 John 4:18.

Jesus gives us instructions on how to have healthy interactions with others as we embrace our femininity and live in freedom. In Matthew 10:16, He tells His disciples that He is sending them "out as sheep in the midst of wolves." Jesus advised them to "be wise as serpents and harmless as doves." This scripture is clear: there are individuals in this world who have a wolf-like mentality. They want to destroy us! Instead of fearing these people or allowing them to control or manipulate us, we must use humility and wisdom. The dove represents humility. In our relationships with others, we should never provoke anyone to anger or conflict.

The serpent represents wisdom. As serpents, we should never unduly expose ourselves to abuse or mistreatment. If you are ever in a situation where your wellbeing is at risk, **get help**. If you are currently in an abusive situation know that it is not God's will for you to be in any relationship where you are being misused or taken advantage of. Move swiftly and get help now.

2.   *Surround yourself with support*

    Once you've changed your perspective, it's time to evaluate your circle. If your inner circle doesn't have your best interests at heart, it will be difficult to maintain a new perspective of freedom. Therefore, surround yourself with individuals who are willing to walk alongside you and support you on your journey of healing. These individuals may be spiritual advisors, teachers, mothers and mother-figures, friends, etc. Also consider seeking the help of a mental health professional to get to the root of the trauma you've experienced. One of the best decisions I made on my healing journey was committing to counseling.

    Some of you may have the mindset I once had regarding counseling, as I thought it was worthless and ineffective. I talked myself out of going to counseling many times because I felt like counselors were only doing their job to get paid and weren't really concerned about the real trauma that I was experiencing! It wasn't until a therapist came to my church and shared the benefits of counseling that I decided to give it a shot. I could relate to some of the terms she described, like post-traumatic stress disorder or PTSD. I thought maybe God was offering me some tangible help for my healing journey.

Honestly, my first counseling experience was not good at all. My counselor didn't seem very interested in her job or helping me to be free. A few months later, she was no longer working at the practice! My second counselor helped me a lot, and her advice was life changing. I stopped going to her, however, when she fell asleep during one of our sessions!

I share these experiences to keep it real. Don't let them deter you, though, because I didn't let them deter me. No one is perfect. Counselors are human too. Sometimes, you have to eat the meat and spit out the bones. Just don't let anything stop you from getting the help you need. Be open and willing to change! If one therapist doesn't work, try someone else. Finding a counselor you feel comfortable with in your journey of healing is key. Take your time, don't rush the process, and find the counselor who is the best fit for you.

Another thing to remember is that consistency is key. When someone has a goal of losing weight, she can't go to the gym once every three months and expect to meet her goal. This is unrealistic. One of the mistakes I made in the beginning of my healing journey was that I stopped going to counseling when things in my life got better. Weeks later, I regressed, and I was back at square one. I also stopped going whenever I had tough discussions about my traumatic experiences. My counselor would say something I wasn't ready to receive, and I shut down. I wouldn't return to counseling for months!

Don't do this! Stay the course! Remember that healing depends on our choices. Make a conscious decision to see a counselor once a week. If you're able, commit to counseling for at least one year straight. Even when you feel like nothing is changing, keep going! When you start discussing hard areas and hear hard truths, don't stop. The real you, the free you, will thank you in the long run, and the effects of your decision will be eternally evident.

3. *Choose to let go*

As you seek to surround yourself with support, you will realize that some things and people are a hindrance to your freedom. In that case, you must choose to let go! Letting go can be difficult, but it is one of the most fruitful things we can do for ourselves and those around us. If you want to embrace your femininity, you must release your old self and old way of responding. Life will always give us reasons to be depressed and stressed out; nevertheless, we must learn the art of letting go. Refuse to worry about things you have no control over and commit to a life of grace and peace.

Think about one person you're very close to. This could be your close friend or even a family member. Does this person add or take away joy? After being in this person's presence, do you feel more or less at peace? When you're talking to this person on the phone are you energized, or do you feel depleted? These are the kinds of questions to ask yourself as you evaluate your personal relationships. You must actively let go of the toxic people in your life. Some associations can invite anxiety and depression into our lives. This is something I learned the hard way! Some relationships need to end altogether, while others need healthy boundaries applied. No matter the case, know that it is okay for you to adjust your friendships and relationships for the sake of peace and growth.

4.   *Use what you have*

Sometimes we think we need more than what we have to facilitate our healing. You may not have the finances you want or a large support system to rely on. The truth is, however, that everything you possess right now is all you need to get started! Work with what you've been given, and exhaust all possibilities, even ones you might be overlooking. You may not have the money to hire Iyanla Vanzant for counseling, but do you have insurance to see a local counselor? You may not have encouragement from certain friends or family members, but can you join a support group on Facebook? Help is available! And if you are ready and willing to put in the work, God is faithful to give you all the things you need "that pertain to life and godliness" (2 Pet. 1:3).

5.   *Give yourself grace*

Another crucial step in the healing process is to remember you are human. Therefore, healing won't take place overnight. It is a lifelong journey. Give yourself grace throughout this process. Each time you make a mistake, learn from it. Forgive yourself. Create boundaries, so that you don't repeat the same mistake. Whatever you must do to keep learning and growing, do it.

As I mentioned in the previous chapter, the women in my family have experienced generational trauma, and it has affected the way we parent. It was more natural for me to be emotionally unavailable towards my children than it was for me to be present with them in the moment. I was determined to break this generational cycle of parenting trauma, but I had to give myself grace in the process. There were great days, and there were, what I call, "learning" days. Whenever I had a learning day, which I still experience, I first reminded myself that God is pleased with the fact that I'm doing my best. I give myself time and grace to recover from that experience. Then, I develop a strategy to do better next time. Don't beat yourself up when you make a mistake; instead, give yourself grace and strive to become better.

6. *Never stop learning*

Learn, learn, learn! Even after reading this book, gain more knowledge on womanhood and femininity. Never stop learning. There is always room for growth. There are two books that have been extremely beneficial throughout my healing journey. Myles Munroe's *Understanding the Purpose and Power of Woman* goes in depth about the specific purpose God has for women, and it has drastically changed my life! Another great book I recommend is *The Rules of Engagement* by Dr. Cindy Trimm. This book teaches you how to use the power of prayer to shift atmospheres and perspectives. I recommend this book to everyone, whether you consider yourself a veteran or beginner when it comes to prayer. Everything that manifests in the tangible realm is a direct result of what happens in the spiritual realm. If we are going to recover from trauma and embrace our femininity, we must learn how to pray effectively; this book will teach you how to do that.

In addition to resources, make sure you position yourself to learn from people who are where you want to be, not where you've been. I did this very practically by joining a body of believers, specifically praying women, who supported me throughout my journey. I attended a church where the authentic Word of God was being taught, and I was able to grow. Ask God to send teachers and models to glean from! Jesus wants you to be healed, and I am a witness that He is faithful to do it if you ask Him.

As you continue to learn, let me provide a word of caution: be careful about the information you absorb. Everything you read about femininity may not be coming from a pure or wise source. For this reason, a safe place to begin is by studying some of the women in the Bible, such as Rahab, Esther and Mary, the mother of Jesus. These are women we can glean from as we seek to understand and embrace our femininity. In the next chapter, we will examine a Biblical model of the feminine woman and learn how we can apply lessons from her life to our own.

4

Life Through the Lens of a Feminine Woman: Proverbs 31 Study

Who are we meant to be as women? I asked myself this question after I made the conscious decision to live in freedom. I soon realized that the best way to find the answer to this question is to ask my Creator. If our car breaks down, do we take it to the grocery store to get fixed? Absolutely not! We take it to a dealership or to someone who has enough knowledge to repair it, right? The same is true with our identities as women. Trauma causes a breakdown in our identities, and God is the only one with enough knowledge to fix our broken pieces. If we want to be *fixed*—to truly understand who we're meant to be—we must go to our Creator and discover His original intent for our lives.

One of the most beautifully written passages about womanhood and femininity can be found in Proverbs 31:10-31. Read this passage below from the New Living Translation. It is entitled "A Wife of Noble Character:"

Who can find a virtuous and capable wife? She is more precious than rubies. Her husband can trust her, and she will greatly enrich his life. She brings him good, not harm, all the days of her life. She finds wool and flax and busily spins it. She is like a merchant's ship, bringing her food from afar. She gets up before dawn to prepare breakfast for her household and plan the day's work for her servant girls.

She goes to inspect a field and buys it; with her earnings she plants a vineyard. She is energetic and strong, a hard worker. She makes sure her dealings are profitable; her lamp burns late into the night.

Her hands are busy spinning thread, her fingers twisting fiber. She extends a helping hand to the poor and opens her arms to the needy. She has no fear of the winter for her household, for everyone has warm clothes. She makes her own bedspreads. She dresses in fine linen and purple gowns.

Her husband is well known at the city gates, where he sits with other civic leaders. She makes belted linen garments and sashes to sell to the merchants. She is clothed with strength and dignity, and she laughs without fear of the future. When she speaks, her words are wise, and she gives instructions with kindness.

She carefully watches everything in her household and suffers nothing from laziness. Her children stand and bless her. Her husband praises her: "There are many virtuous and capable women in the world, but you surpass them all!"

Charm is deceptive, and beauty does not last; but a woman who fears the Lord will be greatly praised. Reward her for all she has done. Let her deeds publicly declare her praise.

In this chapter, we will dissect the above passage of scripture. Verse-by-verse, we will study the traits of the ultimate feminine woman: the Proverbs 31 Woman. Then, I will share how you can apply these verses to fully embrace your God-given femininity. Are you excited to live a life of freedom? To gain the knowledge and tools you need to embrace your femininity? Are you ready? Let's go!

Who can find a virtuous and capable wife? She is more precious than rubies.

The word virtuous in this text comes from the Hebrew word *Chayil*, which means strong in all moral and mental qualities. [7] According to this verse, a healed, feminine woman is strong in her morals and mentality. This kind of woman is invaluable. Ruth is a biblical figure who exemplifies this Hebrew word. Ruth experienced a great tragedy when her husband passed away. Instead of going back to her hometown, she chose to stay with mother-in-law Naomi and serve her mother-in-law's God—the true and living God (Ruth 1:16). While Ruth was gleaning stalks of grain, she gained favor from the owner of the field, Boaz, a relative of her father-in-law, Elimelech (Ruth 2:3). In Biblical times, it was acceptable for a relative to marry a widow and become her covering, and Boaz qualified to be her redeemer because of blood relation. However, there was someone who was more qualified because he was a closer relative, so Boaz could not immediately take her as his wife. In Ruth 3:11, Boaz tells Ruth not to worry about a thing, because he will do what is necessary to take care of her. It's in this very same verse that Boaz tells Ruth everyone in town knew she was a virtuous woman.

This word virtuous in the book of Ruth comes from the same Hebrew word *Chayil* found in Proverbs 31:10. Ruth had plenty of opportunities to go after many young men who showed interest in her, but she refused them all. One of the reasons Boaz called Ruth virtuous was because she chose to remain a widow, which, in the Jewish culture, showed proof of purity. It was because of Ruth's strong morals and mentality that Boaz chose her to be his wife. How can we become like Ruth? Take the necessary steps to get well and establish what your morals are in life. Create positive and wise boundaries and stand firm in your morals no matter what society deems right or wrong.

Her husband can trust her, and she will greatly enrich his life.

I believe this scripture and the rest of this passage not only applies to married women, but also to women as a whole. Ask yourself this question: are you trustworthy? It's easy to point the finger and explain all the reasons why someone else can't be trusted, but what about us? The feminine woman is reliable and dependable; she is honest, and she walks in truth. What truths have you been avoiding? What lies have you been telling yourself or others? Make a conscious effort to keep your commitments and strive to follow through on your promises. No one is perfect, but every day we can attempt to be better than we were the day before.

The second portion of this scripture says the Proverbs 31 Woman greatly enriches the life of her husband. Are you enriching the lives of those around you? Are you creating an atmosphere that enhances the people you influence? In order to positively impact others, we must relinquish a selfish mindset. In order to do this, we esteem others more than ourselves. We become great listeners, focusing on what someone else is sharing with us rather than thinking of a quick response. We refuse to be self-serving, concerned only about ourselves and the things we need. We learn how to be servants and care for the needs of others just as we would our own. Everyone around us should feel enriched by our presence.

She brings him good, not harm, all the days of her life.

Are you a person who strives to do good each day, or are you someone who manipulates and exploits those around you? Gossiping, backbiting, and attempting to control people are a few ways we can be harmful to others. If you identify as someone who gossips or backbites (which is speaking negatively about someone when they are not present), you can choose to take on a new identity of love.

In the New Living Translation, 1 Corinthians 13:5-7 tells us that "love is not…rude. It does not demand its own way." It is not irritable, and it keeps no record of being wronged. It does not rejoice about injustice but rejoices whenever the truth wins out. Love never gives up, never loses faith, and is always hopeful, and endures through every circumstance." Taking on the identity of love means refusing to be a part of (including listening to) any conversation that does not exhort or positively esteem another person. Not having pure and genuine intentions is also hurtful. Doing good to others should not be conditional or based on the actions of those particular people. The feminine woman is always benevolent simply because it is the right thing to do.

She finds wool and flax and busily spins it.

The Amplified Bible says, "she looks for wool and flax and works with willing hands in delight." This shows us that the feminine woman uses the resources she already has. We can complain about not having time, resources, or help to pursue our goals or we can be like the Proverbs 31 Woman and *find* what we need! As I mentioned in the previous chapter, everything required for growth and healing is available to us. Whether you have a little or a lot right now, use what you have! Use your creativity to move forward and become the person you want to be.

She is like a merchant's ship, bringing her food from afar.

This verse shows us that the feminine woman is hard-working, and she isn't afraid to put in time and effort. It shows that she's connected to people and places beyond her own neighborhood. This woman is strategic, and the advancement of her household is her motivation. She isn't afraid to pursue distant, advantageous opportunities, and she can bring in from afar what is necessary to supply her household.

How can we be more like the Proverbs 31 Woman from this verse? Don't expect everything to come easy. You must be willing to put in the time and effort necessary to see your dreams manifest. Break out from what's familiar and be willing to connect with others outside of your community. Always approach new places and environments with a servant's mindset—look for ways to add value. When an opportunity presents itself, don't be afraid to take calculated risks for honest profit and advancement. Chase after your goals even if the territory in which you are walking in is foreign.

She gets up before dawn to prepare breakfast for her household and plan the day's work for her servant girls.

We can clearly see that the Proverbs 31 Woman is not lazy, and she is not a victim of idleness. She is dutiful and considerate of not only her household, but also those who serve her. Time is the most precious tool in the world. It's something that we cannot buy, and once it is gone, it cannot be retrieved. Learn how to manage your time effectively in such a capacity that you bless your household *and* those around you! Establish your priorities and create healthy boundaries to increase your productivity. Let go of things that deplete your energy so that you can devote time to what really matters in life.

She goes to inspect a field and buys it; with her earnings she plants a vineyard.

The feminine woman knows how to be creatively strategic with multiplication in mind. This woman invests in real estate and multiplies her earnings. This scripture does not just apply to the businesswoman or the professional woman, but it is also applicable to the stay-at-home mom! If you are a mother, you know that moms must be strategic while raising our children so that we can see growth in the health, education, and overall development of our kids. When we think about our investments of time, emotions, resources, etc., we must always have multiplication in mind. We should never do something for the sake of doing it. On the contrary, we must expect a multiplied harvest!

She is energetic and strong, a hard worker.

Most of us are not strong or energetic because of poor eating habits. We love to eat! Food has become our comfort. We eat when we're happy and when we're depressed. We get excited when we're invited to events with free food. We flat out love to eat! It's satisfying to our flesh. But this is the reality: if we are going to be intentional about living free and embracing our femininity, we must change our eating habits. We must learn how to eat healthy. It's necessary!

Apostle Marcus Taylor taught me that food is information, and everything we eat is either telling our body to live or die. This statement was mind blowing to me, because I never thought of food in this manner. We can't produce, nurture, or creatively multiply anything if we do not have the energy to do so. Part of the depression, anxiety, fatigue, and dysfunctionality we experience as a disempowered woman is because of our eating habits. So, what do we do?

Start small. Start by making one healthy choice a day. Don't condemn yourself for your previous eating habits. Now that you know food communicates information to your body, you are accountable for your choices from here on out. Choose to bake chicken instead of frying it. Eat grapes and raw veggies for a snack instead of the cake and ice cream in the fridge. You can also fast at least once a week to cleanse your body of unhealthy toxins. Apostle Marcus Taylor's beautiful wife, Pastor Sha'Da Taylor, taught me the 80%-20% strategy. As you seek to improve your eating habits, as I am every day, strive to make 80% of your diet healthy foods and 20% unhealthy foods. Teach your children to do the same! Your health and long life will thank you.

She makes sure her dealings are profitable; her lamp burns late into the night.

The feminine woman is filled with joy and comfort in the success of her labor. Celebrate your successes and your improvements! Celebrate every step you take in the right direction. Know that every bit of work you do is effectual—bringing about your ultimate success as a feminine woman. We see, again, in the second portion of this scripture that the feminine woman does not give way to idleness even in the darkness of night. Stay watchful and cautious. Maintain the wellness of your household and environment and use discernment to ensure a healthy balance.

Her hands are busy spinning thread, her fingers twisting fiber.

The feminine woman stays efficient, and she knows how to get things done. One of the things that I received from this verse is to do away with procrastination. I am not suggesting that you keep busy like a chicken with its head cut off. Conversely, I *am* suggesting that you learn how to use your time effectively. The feminine woman cannot afford to give into laziness or procrastination. All of creation is waiting for us (Romans 8:19).

> ***She extends a helping hand to the poor and opens her arms to the needy.***

Charity and generosity are the essence of who the feminine woman is. She is merciful and benevolent. As feminine women, we love God and His people, especially those who are poor or in need. Our femininity is expressed in our willingness to lend a helping hand whenever it's within our capacity. It's just who we are! These acts of generosity and kindness are both big and small. For some of us, we must be intentional with our kindness.

Let there be no condemnation for the woman who is used to withholding her time, kind words, energy, or resources, because freedom is available to you now. Start by doing one kind or generous thing for someone once a week. "The race is not given to the swift, nor the battle to the strong" (Eccles. 9:11). Victory belongs to those who turn away from doing wrong and live righteously. The more we practice choosing our words carefully and being kind to others, the more it will become an effortless part of who we are!

She has no fear of the winter for her household, for everyone has warm clothes.

The King James Version of the Bible states, "She is not afraid of the snow for her household: for all her household are clothed in scarlet." I used to recite this verse in my prayers as a declaration of God's promise to me, and I want to declare it over you: you and your household are dressed in scarlet, and you will have no need to be afraid of the winter! A winter season can symbolize a period of lack. It's a season that appears to be bare, and there are no obvious signs of growth to the natural eye. In biblical times, scarlet was often associated with wealth, and being dressed in scarlet shows us that the Proverbs 31 Woman is always well prepared for the winter. When I prayed this scripture, I was reminding God of His promise (because the word of God is a book filled with His promises toward us, and He is faithful to His promises). Since I am a virtuous woman, like the woman in this passage, I declared that I would not fear potential lack and all of my household would be taken care of.

What does this mean for you? You must always be prepared for the winter seasons of life. In addition to preparedness, have faith! Winter seasons may seem unfruitful, but God will cause whatever you give Him to multiply. Also, use wisdom when you are experiencing times of abundance. I encourage you to read the story of Joseph. Using the wisdom of God, he strategically saved all of Egypt from the famine they were experiencing (Gen. 41:53-57). Be strategic and plan not only for the winter season, but also for future generations. What are you leaving behind for your legacy? I encourage you to read the book *Rich Dad, Poor Dad* by Robert Kiyosaki. Invest in your education and learn how to budget and invest. Our world recently experienced a global health pandemic where many lost their jobs, homes, and even lives. Feminine women take the time to plan ahead, so that we are prepared for any winter season!

She makes her own bedspreads. She dresses in fine linen and purple gowns.

The feminine woman has style, y'all! She takes great care of her appearance. It is very essential for us to work on ourselves inwardly, but it is also important for us to maintain our outward appearance. As feminine women, we take delight in caring for ourselves and having great hygiene. I love fashion, and I love looking good! Don't be ashamed of wanting to have a great physical appearance. There is nothing wrong with that. The problem comes when we become self-absorbed, and we esteem our physical appearance more than our inward beauty.

This scripture says that this feminine woman is dressed in fine linen and purple gowns. Purple symbolizes royalty, so this teaches us that we should not be afraid of wanting to have the finer things in life. For those of us who have been saved and blood washed by Jesus, we know that our Father owns everything. What rich father wouldn't want their children to have the best of the best? Matthew 7:11 says "if you then, being evil, know how to give good gifts to your children, how much more will your Father who is in heaven give good things to those who ask Him!" If you want the finer things in life, make wise decisions with your resources. Pursue wealth with fire, zeal, and determination.

Her husband is well known at the city gates, where he sits with other civic leaders.

As a wife, the feminine woman is so loving, kind, generous, and nurturing that she creates an atmosphere conducive for her husband's growth and prosperity. This leads to a positive reputation in public. One of the great privileges of a wife is to assist her husband in achieving his goals (we will dive more deeply into this in chapter nine). The husband in this scripture was not only respected because of his position, but he was also respected because of the virtuous femininity of his wife! For those of us who are single right now, our focus is to create an atmosphere conducive for the growth of our family, friends, and loved ones.

She makes belted linen garments and sashes to sell to the merchants.

Feminine Woman: put your talents in the marketplace! It does not matter if you are a stay-at-home mom, businesswoman, or career-switcher. We all have gifts and talents that can be used to advance humanity forward. There is prosperity attached to your gifts!

> ***She is clothed with strength and dignity, and she laughs without fear of the future.***

This scripture refers to the character of the feminine woman, and it's one of my favorite scriptures. According to the Oxford Dictionary, strength is defined as "the capacity of an object or substance to withstand great force or pressure." Feminine woman, you are clothed with strength! Everything you have been through has shaped and molded you for greatness. You have been strategically chosen for this journey, so that you can share your story with others and help them achieve freedom.

Your resilience and ability to keep going is inspiring. You keep going even when the going gets tough, because you are clothed in strength! As feminine women, we have grit. We keep moving forward even when we feel the pressures of life. The pressure is not sent to break us, but rather clothe us with more strength. Because we are prepared for our winter seasons, we can laugh like the Proverbs 31 Woman without fear of the future.

I want to pause here for a moment to tell you how proud I am of your willingness to embrace your femininity. If you're feeling overwhelmed, take a break from reading. Make a list of three new things you can start doing today based on the lessons you've learned so far. Don't forget to celebrate yourself for every step you take in the right direction.

When she speaks, her words are wise, and she gives instructions with kindness.

Here is another essential principle we must intentionally practice: self-control. Many men will attest to the fact that a woman who uses extreme, harsh language is unattractive. As feminine women, we are mindful of the words we speak. Cursing at anyone is not a part of our vernacular. A tongue full of negativity or complaints is not a part of our vernacular. We always speak words of life. We speak the truth in a loving way, especially if we are given constructive criticism or chastisement. Trust me, I understand that this is easier said than done. But as the old saying goes, if you don't have anything good to say, don't say anything at all!

The King James Version says, "her tongue is a law of kindness." This tells us that our kindness is not optional! The thing about laws is that we are required to obey them no matter the season. If the speed limit is thirty-five miles per hour, we are expected to obey that traffic law whether it's winter, spring, fall, or summer (of course we may have to slow down according to weather conditions, but even in that case, we are expected not to exceed the speed). The law of kindness is bound in the tongue of the feminine woman. No matter how someone may treat us, we speak with kindness. We must be gracious and even-tempered in all our ways. Master the art of having a meek and quiet spirit.

She carefully watches everything in her household and suffers nothing from laziness.

As feminine women, we are great stewards of our household, making sure that everything is headed in the right direction. Note: the married feminine woman is not the head of her household. Her careful watch over her home is necessary for creating an environment for growth and development. It is necessary, and this role cannot be overlooked or replaced. The maturation of her husband and children are dependent on it. It is the duty of the single feminine woman to maintain the wellness of her household as well.

What does this look like practically? As women we have the keen ability to identify what's needed for the betterment of our family and inner circle. Maintaining the wellness of our household means doing what's within our power to propel our families forward. It could come in the form of preparing a meal, doing laundry, teaching, cleaning, and more! Whatever the need may be, it is our responsibility to fulfill it to the best of our ability without laziness or procrastination.

Her children stand and bless her. Her husband praises her:

God has called us to raise our children in a godly way. They must see a loving, committed relationship between us and our Creator. The feminine woman guides her children so that they can navigate life with efficiency and wisdom. Even if we do not mother biological children, there are children and individuals all around us who can benefit from our motherly guidance. As you make the life-changing decisions necessary for freedom, you will impact others in such a way that they will praise your works and call you blessed!

There are many virtuous and capable women in the world, but you surpass them all!

Freedom in our femininity is a lifestyle of power. The more we embrace femininity, the less we identify with the disempowered woman. Excellence follows femininity! Prepare to excel in every area of your life: as a woman, mother, wife, businesswoman, but, most of all, as a woman of God.

Charm is deceptive, and beauty does not last; but a woman who fears the Lord will be greatly praised.

Outward beauty fades with time. The physical appearance of the feminine woman is not her main priority. Our true beauty—our essence—is found in our fear of the Lord. This fear of the Lord is not a terrifying fear, but rather a holy awe of God. Our reverence for the Lord is what gives us the power to embrace femininity. It doesn't matter if you don't know the Lord or if it has been a while since you've talked to Him. Know that Jesus stands at the door of your heart, always knocking and wanting to have an intimate relationship with you (Rev. 3:20). It doesn't matter what you've done in your past or what mistakes you've made.

Jesus loves us. He desperately wants a relationship with us. So much so, that He came off His glorious throne and put on flesh to die just for you and me! He did this so that the filthiness of our sin would no longer keep us from having a relationship with Him. The best part is that He rose from the grave with all power in His hands. This power is the same power that lies within you, and just as He rose from the dead, we, too, can rise out of every bit of bondage that holds us down. When we accept Jesus into our hearts, we are enabled to live in freedom. We have the power to embrace who He originally created us to be as feminine women of the Most High God!

Reward her for all she has done. Let her deeds publicly declare her praise.

Every decision of integrity you make and every step forward you take will be rewarded with fruitfulness. Know that even the things that you do for others in private will be rewarded publicly. Embracing our femininity should be a daily goal and, ultimately, the essence of who we are.

~~~

Although written many years ago, the principles of this passage are timeless and apply to every woman on earth today. Start small, and intentionally apply the lessons from this chapter. I guarantee your life will never be the same again!

5

The Power of Vulnerability: Forgiveness within the Healing Process

To be honest, out of all the chapters in this book, this one was the hardest to write. Every chapter represents a season of life I've been through. For this particular chapter, I had to go back inside of myself and uproot everything I so desperately tried to brush under my mental rug. The words on these pages are not just opinions—these are trials I've had to journey through and lessons I've learned in the process. I have experienced so many hurts. I've been raped, abused, manipulated, lied to, and discriminated against. My metamorphosis into a feminine woman first began with a revelation of what it truly meant to be vulnerable, understanding the power of vulnerability, and going through the process of forgiveness. This is the healing chapter for me.

Physical, emotional, and financial abuse teaches us that vulnerability is negative. Heartbreak and rejection enter our hearts when certain people in our lives *should* protect us, but they don't. It could have been an absent parent or a disconnected spouse. Whatever the case, the result is our unwillingness to ever be vulnerable again. However, if we are going to live in freedom and embrace our femininity, we must become comfortable with vulnerability.

When many people hear the word vulnerability, they automatically think of weakness. I thought the same way. According to the Oxford Dictionary, vulnerability means "to be open to attack or harm; to be easily attacked or harmed." In other words, vulnerability requires openness. I encourage you to shift the way you perceive vulnerability. Vulnerability is not a bad thing! Being vulnerable as a feminine woman means letting your guard down with wisdom and allowing yourself to freely give and receive love.

For a long time, I struggled with the fear of rejection. I'm naturally a very loving and caring person. Love just bubbles up inside of me. I enjoy encouraging and complimenting others, and I'm a hugger. However, I was afraid to be my true self around others because of the negativity I experienced in the past. I entertained the negative things people said about me and feared someone would think I was "doing too much." I didn't want my love to be rejected. I started to believe my kind words meant nothing to people and weren't worth sharing. All these thoughts were lies, and the enemy is, indeed. "a liar and the father of [lies]" (John 8:44). He is "the accuser of our brethren" (Rev. 12:10).

What I didn't realize is that hiding myself from the world was only making things worse. My relationships started deteriorating, and I found myself losing valuable people in my life. This caused me to fall into a deep depression. I was out of touch with my body and mind because I wasn't being the authentic, feminine woman God created me to be.

Vulnerability requires a determination to be your authentic self no matter who's around. Don't worry about who does or doesn't like the real you. God made you the feminine woman that He did because the world needs to experience you! All of creation needs you to be your authentic self because you will bless the lives of those who are connected to you. Your true friends will love you. Your divine tribe will embrace who you really are. No longer will we dim our light so that others will feel less intimidated. No longer will we put on a facade to impress those around us. No longer will we hold back our love in an effort to shield ourselves from pain. It's time to be free!

Some of you have been afraid to be joyful because you've been surrounded by miserable people. I encourage you to bask in your joy. Woman, live in that joy! Stop allowing the negative perspectives and opinions of others to bring you into their misery. Have you heard of the phrase "misery loves company?" It's true, and it's time to surround yourself with a different kind of company! Pursue relationships with individuals who give you the space to be joyfully vulnerable, and don't be afraid to love some family members from a distance.

A critical component in the healing process is forgiveness. We must forgive the people who hurt us in the past. Some of us have prematurely written people off when God wanted us to reconcile the relationship (friendships, siblings, etc.). Please do not misunderstand me: there are some people who threaten our physical safety and mental wellbeing, so they *should* be cut off. However, there are other people we choose to cut off because it's easier for us to never speak to them again than to forgive and reconcile. These are the people I'm referring to. These people could be friends, family members, pastors/church members or even coworkers.

My experience with this was not easy, and I could not have done it without the help of The Lord! I had a particular family member that was very negative and verbally abusive to me as a child. She would accuse me of outrageous things and speak curses over my life that I had to fight to overcome as an adult. Every attempt to try to reconcile with this family member always seemed to end in failure. I found myself stepping out of godly character and responding to certain comments or gestures in a very unhealthy way. Soon, I resorted to acting as if this loved one didn't exist. I even felt a sense of false peace—it seemed like everything was just better this way. However, deep down, I knew God wanted this relationship to be reconciled.

The first thing I did was give it to God, and this is the first step in the process of forgiveness. We must first surrender our offender and our broken connection to him or her. Take your hands off it and resist the need to control the situation. Give it completely to God and allow Him to have His way!

Next, we must make the decision to forgive. Forgiveness is not a feeling; it's a choice. One day, you may have a desire to forgive. You've got tears running down your face, and you passionately declare, "I forgive you!" And the next day, you see the person who has hurt you and a feeling of heaviness and anger rises in your chest. Feelings are temporary, and they are not a good indicator of whether or not you've truly forgiven someone. Make the decision today to forgive the people who have offended you. Ask God to help you! He is our loving Father, and He is the "God of all comfort" (2 Cor. 1:3). He longs for you to ask Him for His help and guidance.

Even God, the Creator of heaven and earth, had to forgive. He left His perfect throne, put on flesh and blood and came into a sinful world that had forsaken Him. He allowed His creation to beat, torture, and spit on Him knowing He had the power to call down "legions of angels" to wipe out the entire earth in a fraction of a second (Matt. 26:53). He allowed us to crucify Him so we could have the opportunity to come to Him. He did this so that all who wanted could be saved from damnation. He fulfilled the requirements of God's law by shedding His own blood. Now, fallen creation can have a relationship with the Almighty God. What a mighty God we serve! Hallelujah! He died because He knew you and I would never be holy enough to deserve a relationship with Him. And while they beat and tortured Jesus, He said, "Father, forgive them, for they do not know what they do" (Luke 23:34).

This must be our mindset as we make the decision to forgive those who hurt us: we forgive others because God forgave us (Eph. 4:32). You may say to yourself, *I wasn't living in biblical times. If I was, I would have never done the terrible things those people did to him.* Allow me to enlighten you. Every time you've sinned, every time you've rolled a blunt or gotten drunk, every time you lied or gossiped or even ran a red light, you were crucifying Him. He died because of sin, which means that every time you sin, it's as if you're spitting on Him. The reality is we all fall short of His glory, but He chose to forgive us—He chose to do what was necessary to reconcile us back to the Father. And He has given us the power to reconcile.

Therefore, as feminine women, we forgive those who have offended, oppressed and abused us in any way. We take on the mindset and power of Christ, knowing that they know not what they do. Even if what happened to you was intentional, such a rape or emotional abuse, if the abuser had the capacity to understand what they were doing, they would not have done it. Regardless of the situation, we are called to forgive.

Forgiveness can be very difficult. I had to say out loud *I forgive such and such by faith* every time the offense came to mind. Another strategy I found effective was praying for the person. I encourage you to read *The Bait of Satan* by John Bevere.

Genuinely pray for the person you need to forgive. Pray for them like you would pray for yourself! When I was going through the process of forgiving my ex-husband, my initial prayers were that of revenge: *Lord convict his soul* and *you said you would curse those that curse me, so let everything in his life dry up*. These were also the type of prayers I prayed about the family member God wanted me to reconcile with. My mindset was off, and this type of praying can quickly turn into witchcraft. Though God did not lead me to reconcile with my ex for the sake of marriage, he did want reconciliation for a healthy co-parenting relationship. I could not have that if I continued to pray in this manner. As the Lord rebuked me and taught me how to pray for those who had wronged me, my heart and perspective changed!

I started praying and speaking blessings over their health and mind. I prayed for their salvation, their children, and their legacy. The Lord was healing my heart! He removed my heart of stone and gave me a heart full of compassion and love. If you are open and willing, He will do the same for you no matter the hurt, abuse, or offense that's been inflicted upon you. Give it to God in prayer!

After praying for my family member often, God released me to go directly to her. But it wasn't so that I could tell her all the things she had done to me. Rather, it was to serve her. I served by pouring out my love, being my authentic self in her presence and helping her however I could. This is where I found the power of vulnerability, and, to the glory of God, the relationship was reconciled. This was not an easy thing to do, but I want you to know that with the help of the Holy Spirit, it's possible. Forgiveness allowed me to move forward in healing and freedom.

As you experience the freedom that comes with forgiveness, I want you to be on alert for a potential threat to your progress: defense mechanisms. The Oxford dictionary defines a defense mechanism as "an automatic reaction of the body against disease-causing organisms." Another definition is "a mental process (e.g., repression or projection) initiated, typically unconsciously, to avoid conscious conflict or anxiety." Just as scars are still present after a wound has healed, so can triggers be present after emotional healing. If we are triggered, we may revert back to the defense mechanisms we used in the past: shutting down, controlling, and wearing a mask.

Be aware of your triggers! Triggers are anything that brings you back to the place of victimization and reminds you of the trauma you experienced. Triggers can be places, words, feelings, people or personality types. We must know our triggers and develop a system of processing them. If not, we will continue to identify as a wounded female and interact with others from a disempowered place.

So how do you know if you're experiencing triggers?

- Do you find yourself sad or anxious when you get around a particular person, place, or group of people?
- Do you often have an attitude or negative response when confronted with certain topics, criticism, questions, or conversations?
- Are you often in fight mode when someone tries to hug or touch you in an appropriate way?

If you said yes to any of the questions above, you are experiencing triggers. There are many things that can trigger the place of trauma we are striving to heal from. When this happens, it is our responsibility to identify the trigger and process the emotions in order to continue the healing process. I highly suggest you surround yourself with a great support system and find a counselor who can help you process these emotions. Consider keeping a journal or notebook. Write about any moments you feel yourself reverting to old behaviors. This will help you to pinpoint your triggers.

Once we know our triggers, we can set healthy boundaries. These boundaries allow for the healing process to continue. We cannot control other people's actions; however, we *can* control our own. Some of our triggers may be very subtle. They may not seem serious to someone else, but for us, it can potentially cause a major setback. This is why we need to develop a step-by-step process on how we will respond when we are triggered. For me, when I am triggered by my past, I pause and release all my initial thoughts. I think carefully before I speak or make any decisions. I am very intentional about my next move or response.

As we heal from trauma, forgive those who hurt us, and walk in freedom, we must stay mindful of our triggers and have a plan in place that will keep our defense mechanisms in check. Allow God to be your protector! When you choose to be vulnerable and authentic, you will be empowered in a way that you've never been before.

6

It's Okay to be Free Part II: Practical ways to Embrace your Femininity

Many of us are great at retaining information. The problem comes in when it's time to apply that information to our lives so that we can experience results. In this chapter, we will discuss more practical ways to embrace our femininity.

1. Go with the flow!

Attempting to rationalize and control situations is a trauma response. If we have experienced abandonment or a lack of stability in the past, we often develop a desire to control things and rationalize behavior. We become obsessed with knowing the end from the beginning and every detail in between. Embracing our femininity, however, means going with the flow of life even if we don't have all the details. Yes, we want to be wise, but we must be careful not to over strategize or overthink. Overthinking can lead to worry and stress. These negative emotions rob us of creativity, joy, and femininity. Philippians 4:6 tells us "To be anxious for nothing," but instead, pray about everything. We must tell God what we need and thank Him for all He has done. The beauty in being a believer is the fact that we can go to our Father and pray about everything without having to worry about anything!

If you are someone who struggles to go with the flow, I encourage you to pray and allow God to direct your path (Prov. 3:5-6). The more you trust God, the less you trust yourself. Ask God what you should do in every situation, then trust that He will lead you. Once He's shown you what to do, gracefully follow His path. Spend time reading His Word and praying, and His voice will become more and more recognizable. Trust that God has your back, and that He has already ordered your steps (Psalm 37:23). We can rest without worry and go with the flow of life when we follow God's leading and trust Him with the details.

2. Feel emotions without shame!

I used to hate being emotional, and I avoided processing emotions altogether. It didn't matter what emotion it was, even joy or excitement. Remember when I mentioned I had a subconscious belief system that I was unworthy? This affected my ability to feel and process my emotions. I walked around as a disempowered woman, wounded and unwilling to feel anything. But once I learned how to process my emotions and understood the importance of doing so, I became empowered.

Becoming in sync with your body and emotions is crucial to happiness. Rather than bottling them up, allow yourself to feel every emotion without shame. Don't rush the emotions either. Take time to feel each emotion, and plant yourself in reality. If you feel anxiety in your chest or stomach, embrace that feeling instead of ignoring it. Process it and reflect on what caused the anxiety.

Emotions are indicators. They indicate how we feel and alert us to any possible threats. To process your emotions, you first want to label what you are feeling. Are you afraid? Joyful? Anxious? Use a word to describe what or how you are feeling. Then, give yourself time to feel it without judgment. Sit with it for a moment. Next, dig deep to understand why you are feeling the way you are feeling. Who did you just talk to? What were you thinking about? Once you know what's causing the emotion and why you feel the way that you do, you can be strategic and come up with a solution about how to move forward.

3.   Find joy in everything!

It's our responsibility to live in a place of joy no matter what is going on around us. Joy is a direct result of gratitude. Having an attitude of gratitude enables us to appreciate our current circumstances and acknowledge that things could be worse. No matter where we find ourselves in life—whether we've experienced a major setback in business or suffered a loss in our personal lives—we must learn how to be content in all things (Phil. 4:11).

I know for a fact, though, this is not always easy. When I struggled with poverty, it seemed as though all hell was breaking loose! I was looking for a new place of residence for me and my children, but my credit was so poor I couldn't qualify for any decent housing. One day there was a really bad snowstorm in my city. After picking up my children from school, I came home to find that my furnace went out! I thought to myself, it's one thing for my gas to be cut off, but my furnace?! In a snowstorm? It was just unbelievable!

I would be lying if I said I did not feel deep sadness, but quickly the Holy Spirit reminded me of the promises of God. I had a large electric heater in my room that warmed my room to a certain degree, and I was grateful! I was grateful that my children and I had a roof over our heads. I was grateful that we did not have to go to a homeless shelter. The Holy Spirit held me in this moment and reminded me of His promise in Romans 8:28 that "all things work together for good to those who love God, to those who are the called according to His purpose." He reminded me that He is my Jehovah Jireh, and He will supply all of my needs (Phil. 4:19).

A week later, after doing all that He told me to do, God supernaturally made a way for me to move out of my house and into a luxury apartment with a beautiful lake view! God is able, and He is faithful to perform! Hallelujah!

If you are struggling with finding joy in everything, I encourage you to meditate on the fact that things could be worse.

No matter your situation, be grateful for where you are. Find the promises of God pertaining to your specific situation, follow God's lead, and expect for God to show up.

4.   Be present and live in the moment!

Too often we dwell on the past or are so focused on the future that we miss our opportunity to live in the present. Enjoy the beauty of right now! I encourage you to practice what's called grounding. Grounding yourself means using your senses and/or objects around you to keep calm and remain aware of the present moment. One of the main things I do to ground myself is use physical touch. I move my thumb in a light circular motion on the tip of my index finger. It helps tremendously when I am in large crowds because I'm an introvert.

There are other times when I use all of my senses to help ground me. When I feel overwhelmed, I ask myself *what do you see?* Then, I focus on a particular object. *What do you hear? What do you feel? What do you smell? What do you taste?* And I focus on that specific sense. Once I'm finished, I remind myself that I am safe.

Other things you can do to practice being present are long walks, quiet time in a good book, and quality time playing with your children, grandchildren, nieces, or nephews. Focus on one moment at a time by giving your all to that moment without worrying about the next. While you're completing one task, refuse to think about what you need to do next. While you're playing with your children, don't think about what you're going to wear tomorrow. Planning for the future is important, but more than anything else, enjoy the time you've been allotted today because you don't know what day will be your last. As Christ instructs, let tomorrow "worry about its own things," because whatever it may hold, God is already there (Matt. 6:34).

5. **Rid yourself of negative people, places, and things!**

This is something I've discussed in previous chapters, and it is essential to mention it again. Maintaining a positive environment is necessary for you to blossom as the feminine woman you are destined to be. Don't allow guilt to make you feel bad for distancing yourself from negative people, places, and things. It's possible to have someone in your life, and not allow them to negatively influence your spiritual or emotional environment.

One of the greatest lessons I've learned is how to use wisdom in friendships. Apostle Marcus Taylor put it like this: if you have a friendship with someone and she ends up stabbing you in the back by sharing your personal business with everyone, then you have two options: you can either cut this person off or you can love her from a distance. You can remain friends as long as you refrain from sharing your personal business again. You also must use wisdom when it comes to the influence people have on your future. If your friend smokes marijuana and that's a trigger for you, don't hang out with your friend when she smokes. However, if it is too overwhelming and you know the relationship is not making you better, have the courage to let it go.

6. Receive joyfully!

If we've been constantly let down in the past, we often develop *the independent woman* mentality. We handle things on our own, and the last thing we want is to ask for or receive help.

Just like the need to control and rationalize are trauma responses, the inability to receive help, gifts and love are also responses resulting from trauma. Girl, it's time to be free, and let that go! A major part of embracing femininity is learning how to receive joyfully without having to earn it or do something for it.

In the past, if someone gave me a compliment, I felt as if I owed a compliment in return. I found it hard to receive help without having to give something for it. At the time that I'm writing this book, I have three small children. I can remember times when someone would offer to help get my kids out of the car or offer to buy them winter coats. My response was always "no, thanks," in a kind way. I did this because I didn't want to be viewed as a victim. I didn't want people to think I was weak or inadequate. However, this was an unhealthy response.

After becoming aware that the feminine woman is a receiver, I started to change my response from no to yes! At first, I had to force myself to receive help from others. What's amazing, though, is as I did, life became much easier. Many of us can joyfully give, but we are not comfortable with joyfully receiving.

Psalm 23:1 tells us that "The Lord is [our] Shepherd; [we] shall not want." This means He takes great care of us spiritually, emotionally, mentally, and physically. God also sends people to take care of us, and we have to be willing to receive this help with joy and without shame.

The truth is the feminine woman is a receiver. She masters the art of "yes" and "thank you." When someone offers help, practice saying yes. When someone gives you a kind word or compliment, practice saying thank you without feeling obligated to give one in return. Be okay with receiving when the time comes to receive.

7. **Love and accept yourself!**

All of us have flaws. There are things we wish we could change about ourselves. But embracing femininity is about loving and accepting ourselves for who we are. As feminine women, we should always esteem ourselves without becoming vain or overly confident. When you look at your reflection in the mirror, tell yourself that you look good! If there are things you want to change about yourself, change them. And if there are things you cannot change, accept those things by reminding yourself that you are "fearfully and wonderfully made" (Psalm 139:14). Love who you are while working on your personal development daily.

Read books and attend seminars to help you increase your confidence and develop your character. If you want to lose weight, come up with an action plan to reach your goal. Whatever your personal development goals, be sure to love yourself throughout the process. Loving yourself means recognizing your strengths and working to improve your weaknesses. You also love yourself by saying positive affirmations aloud like the ones in chapter three.

8. Practice self-care and maintain your mental health!

My definition of self-care is doing whatever you need to maintain balance within your mind, body, soul, and spirit. Self-care ensures you have enough to give others. This is important because many of us pour and pour, but we forget to take care of ourselves. Pouring from an empty cup will bring about exhaustion, regret, anger, and identity confusion. Some of us aren't taking care of ourselves because we feel guilty doing so.

I used to be the mother who walked out of the store with a ton of things for my children and nothing for myself. I felt so guilty for wanting something for myself as if this desire made me less of a mother. If you can identify with this, sister, let this be the confirmation you need: it is perfectly okay to do things for yourself! You cannot allow any role you play in your life to overshadow who you are as an individual.

Identify what you need to help you feel balanced and whole. Do you need to take a nature walk for 30 minutes a day? Plan more lunch dates with friends? Reflect and write in a journal at the beginning or end of each day? Whatever is needed, do that. My self-care routine includes getting my eyebrows and nails done, treating myself to retail therapy from time to time, and going to brunch with friends. For spiritual self-care, I attend a Holy Spirit filled church with an amazing body of believers. I also attend different seminars and conferences to strengthen my faith.

If you don't take care of yourself, who will? It's important that we set aside time to do things we love. Spend time alone and spend time with friends. Try a new restaurant. Take yourself on a shopping spree (within reason). See a therapist or life coach to nurture your mental health. Don't fall into the trap of saying you're fine when you're really breaking down inside. Don't believe the lie that you have to go through this process of healing alone. Sometimes, reaching out to someone else is the best way to maintain our mental health. Nurture yourself in all the ways you need. Every woman is different, so self-care will look differently in each of our lives. Whatever you deem as self-care, make the time to do that because you are worth the investment.

9. **Slow down!**

We live in a fast-paced society. Our schedules are full of to-dos and deadlines. But we must be intentional about slowing down. Ironically, slowing down helps us to live a stress-free life. I am an absolute cranky pants when I'm rushing or concerned about the million things I have to do. As women, we are more effective when we take our time. What helps me is making sure I give myself enough time to complete tasks, and I'm willing to wake up a little earlier to do this. I also strive to get enough sleep at night so that I wake up refreshed and ready for the day. When we are caught in the trap of busyness, we're unable to live in the present.

Slowing down in my life has been one of the biggest blessings the Lord has given me! We can live in joy when we slow down. We are more peaceful and naturally able to exude our femininity without effort. We don't have to be ruled by anxiety or uneasiness, and we can slow down and enjoy our lives.

10.   Spend time with other women!

Finally, spend time with women who accept you for who you are without judgment. These are women who understand your worth and appreciate your value. When we spend time with other women our femininity is empowered, and we are able to build upon our support systems.

7

Boss Lady: Femininity and the CEO

This chapter is for all the bosses: business owners, female leaders, CEOs, and even aspiring businesswomen. I mentioned earlier in this book that I justified leading others from a masculine core because I knew God called me to be a very wealthy woman and warrior for Him. When I thought about being a businesswoman and all that it would entail, I thought I needed to be dominant and masculine to do so. I had a drill sergeant mentality—things had to be my way! I was precise and determined, filled with perseverance and zeal. I thought I was doing things with excellence. But I was so wrong! It's great to be ambitious and passionate, but what's important is to be the leader God called us to be while embracing femininity instead of rejecting it.

All mankind has both feminine and masculine energy, however, as women, we are designed to live from our feminine core. Focus, planning, and management are the key tasks of a great leader. Both men and women were created to lead (with the male leading as head if you're married), and both have the capacity to do so. The only difference is the way in which we lead.

The key to embracing your femininity as a female leader is balancing both your feminine and masculine energy. Oftentimes as female leaders we become too dominant. We have the need to control everything, and we lose our sensitivity and ability to connect with others in the process. Failing to embrace femininity as a female leader is actually a weakness, and it can cause poor decision making. You'll find yourself competing with others and pushing away your team, customers, clients, and those who may have been sent to help you along the way.

As a feminine leader, our power is in connecting with those around us in an emotional and spiritual way. Listen and get to know everyone who is a part of your team. Listen to their goals and dreams, understand their personality, and get to know their family through conversation. Listen with spiritual and natural ears and use your intuition as well as your intellect. Feel the words your team shares with you and identify with them. Resist the urge to rush. Be present with your team and make good eye contact.

This connection with your team will become the beginning of what is called transformational leadership. This type of leadership not only changes systems, but also the social environment and, ultimately, the lives of those around you. When women lead from a masculine core, we tend to utilize transactional leadership rather than transformational leadership. Both leadership styles are effective to a degree, but as feminine leaders, we strive to connect with those around us on a deeper level to promote transformational change in our organizations and those whom we oversee.

Successful, feminine leaders are humble. They acknowledge their limitations and allow others to assist in those areas. Don't be afraid to admit areas of weakness or inexperience. Vulnerability is strength, and it is a powerful tool for the feminine boss. Be vulnerable and be your authentic self around your team.

In doing so, you will gain the trust of your employees and clients. Allow others to assist you and receive that help joyfully! Pride will bring down your organization while humility will build it up. Welcome feedback and constructive criticism without backlash, retaliation, or offense.

Remember: your job as a feminine leader is to lead people and not dominate them. You are a servant and not a dictator. Nurture the personalities of those around and under you. Help to build their confidence and self-esteem within their roles. Additionally, be sure to show empathy and tolerance. Give criticism from a place of love and concern. When the time comes that you have to let someone go, do so with gentleness and love, and release them honorably.

It is possible to be a phenomenal, female leader without forsaking your feminine core. Transformational leadership is achieved when you embrace what makes you uniquely feminine. Your ability to connect with the people you lead is your strongest asset. Use this as you serve in all the leadership capacities God has blessed you with.

8

Mommy Hen: Femininity and the Single Mother

Mama, I feel you! I am familiar with the stress that comes with being a single mother. I want you to know how awesome you are. Not because you may or may not be doing everything right, but because you're making the decision to be a better woman. For the sacrifices, tears, and adjustments—the things no one knows you've done for your children—woman, I applaud you! You are doing the best you know how to do, and God sees you! You are amazing in His eyes, and you are loved more than you could ever know. Even when you feel alone, know God is beside you. He is assisting you and giving you strength and strategies for the journey.

One life-changing tip that has helped me tremendously as a single mother of three small children is scheduling. *Schedule, schedule, schedule!* A lot of the stress I've experienced as a single parent has come because I didn't have a schedule. Now, children won't always follow the schedule we set, but the more structure we put in place, the less chaotic and stressful our lives will be.

The first thing on your schedule should be to wake up earlier than your children (if you're able to). Even if it's just one hour earlier, waking up early allows you to mentally prepare yourself for the day. Pray, mediate, take a shower, make yourself breakfast and get ready for the day ahead. It is much more difficult to prepare your children for the day when they are waking you up, rather than the other way around. Even if it's uncomfortable at first, stick with it. This simple adjustment will reduce the daily stress that comes with being a single parent. When mama is happy, healthy and refreshed, she is a better mother to her children.

Next, set the rest of the morning schedule for your children. What will you be helping your children do when they first wake up? Schedule things a couple hours before the time you need to leave the house. For instance, if you must leave by 10:00 a.m., start preparing your children's breakfast around 7:00 a.m. (of course this will depend on you and the number of children that you have).

Starting early affords enough time to handle any unexpected things that happen without having to rush. As you implement scheduling, you will discover the timing that works best for you.

Another effective strategy for morning routines is laying with your children and giving hugs and kisses ten minutes before they get out of bed. Children are easier to handle in the morning when they wake up to our love rather than bright lights and commands. This technique is effective for *all* children—everyone benefits from mama's love and affection first thing in the morning.

In addition to a morning schedule, it is also wise to create an evening schedule. Put tasks on your evening schedule that will help make your morning run as smoothly as possible. This includes baths, setting clothes aside, ironing, etc. Doing things in the evening vs. the morning will save you a tremendous amount of time and energy. Additionally, don't forget to make time for you in your schedule. Just because you have children doesn't mean you are no longer an individual person. Make time to do the things you love in life. As you do, you'll find that the happier you are as an individual, the more tolerant and joyful you will be as a parent.

Now we will move from regulating our time to regulating our emotions. This is something dear to my heart, and I'm still learning to master it even as I write this book. As mothers, we must use our emotions as indicators, not dictators, of our actions. For example, let's say you had a bad day, and you're in a bad mood. Despite your rule that drinks aren't allowed outside of the kitchen, your child brings grape juice into the living room and spills it on your freshly cleaned carpet! Oh my! It is natural for you to feel anger, right? And, of course, because you're already in a bad mood, your emotions are intensified. So, you lash out. You yell at your child, maybe even spank her. Now, the child has an emotional scar—not because she didn't listen, but because you allowed your emotions to lead.

Mama, I encourage you not to punish your children while you're angry or full of rage. When you feel overwhelmed as a parent, step away from the situation. Walk somewhere within your house, take a few deep breaths, and calm down. Address the situation when you can handle it appropriately without overreacting or misdirecting your anger. There is a time and a place for a punishment that's appropriate for the infraction. The overall principle here is to learn how to manage your emotions in a healthy way as a single parent. The last thing we want to do is raise children who need to heal from their mother's words or actions.

Another technique that will help you in your motherhood journey is the art of letting go. Let go of everything you don't have control over, especially the father of your child(ren). Stop wasting time regretting the relationship you had with your child's father and choose to move forward. You can't change the past. If nothing else, be grateful that you've been blessed to be a great mother to your amazing child. As single mothers, we must learn how to manage procedures, not people. I learned this concept from Bishop TD Jakes. Many of us are stressed out because we are concerned about what our child's father is or is not doing. Woman, I want you to be free! As a feminine mother, our responsibility is to nurture our children and go with the flow. It is ideal for your child's father to have an active role in his child's life; however, you cannot control or force him to do so. Let go!

Joyfully manage your part in your child's life, and ensure your child knows that he or she is loved, special, and appreciated. If your child's father is not active, ask God to send positive father figures into your children's lives to help in their development. God can raise up positive male figures in your child's life, such as a teacher, boxing coach, youth pastor, mentor etc. Before they were your children, they belonged to God. He is a good Father, and He will make sure they are well taken care of.

Money can be a major stressor for a single mother, but I want to encourage you not to stress over finances. God promised to supply every need you have. Do what you can and be open to increase. If you are not satisfied with where you are mentally, financially, or spiritually, make a plan to get to where you want to be. Know that God sees and hears you, and He is walking with you every step of the way! Everything is going to be alright, and I am a witness of it!

Though being a single parent can be challenging, it is possible for us to thrive in this role. Use these strategies to manage your resources, emotions, and expectations. Focus on your precious children and develop one-on-one relationships with them. Get to know their strengths and weaknesses, and nurture them so that they can be all that God intends them to be on earth. The best thing you can do for your children is what you're already doing—becoming the best mother you can possibly be.

9

Mrs. Right: Femininity and the Married Woman

I have experienced what it's like to be married, and now, I understand what it's like to be divorced. The principles and concepts we will discuss in this chapter are lessons the Lord has revealed during and after my marriage. Some of the things God taught me were like medicine: the pills were hard to swallow but they brought healing to my soul.

I encourage you to allow this chapter to transform your paradigm. Digest these concepts and apply them to your marriage. Some may be familiar to you and others may be foreign. No matter the case, honestly evaluate who you are as a wife and how well you are embracing your femininity within your marriage.

It's nearly impossible to be a healthy, feminine wife if you are not first a healthy, feminine woman. In order for us to serve our husbands in the capacity God intends for us, we first have to be healed. We need to know what it means to be a woman who embraces her femininity as discussed in previous chapters. Failing to do so is one of the major pitfalls that lead to my divorce. This is why I can say with confidence that the principles in this chapter have the capacity to save a marriage!

I am speaking to the married woman from a place of experience. What I'm about to say is in love, gentleness, and sincerity. Woman...

You are not always right.

Too often married women take on the identity of Mrs. Right or Mrs. Always Right. We have sayings like "Happy wife, happy life," which gives off the impression that women are always right. This is so far from the truth! Often, we have a hard time receiving constructive criticism, and we take offense when we are criticized by our husbands. Instead of listening and receiving, we deflect by pointing out their flaws.

Many of us may not have had a great relationship with our biological fathers, or we may not have seen what a healthy marriage looks like. In this case, we don't understand what marriage entails from a biblical perspective. A wife's primary duty is to serve her husband in all capacities. By doing so, we embrace our femininity. We must serve our husbands like we serve Christ. Jesus is our ultimate husband, and He created marriage to reflect our marriage and dedication to Him on the earth. With this in mind, we are to serve and honor our husbands in the same capacity we do Christ (and of course Jesus Christ is always first and Lord of our lives).

One of the reasons we don't serve our husbands is because many of us don't serve Christ. We don't love Him with all our hearts, minds, and souls. We serve Him when it's convenient, and this is the same way we serve our husbands. Service requires selflessness, but many of us serve in a conditional way. We'll help or assist if our husbands are doing certain things for us. This mindset is out of order, and it isn't aligned with God's design for marriage.

As feminine wives and children of the Most High God, our service to our spouses cannot be conditional. We must make the choice to help and serve our husbands no matter the circumstance. We honor them as we honor Christ. To do this, we must let down our walls of defense and become vulnerable. This is not easy, however, with God nothing is impossible! Everything you do for your spouse is for the Lord, and He will reward you for it.

Some of you may be thinking *you don't know my husband! He doesn't appreciate who I am, nor does he acknowledge the things that I do for him.* You are right! I don't know your husband or your situation. I *do* know that God is your greatest defender. Allow the Lord to be your defense and your defender! One thing I know for sure and have witnessed for myself: no sin goes unpunished, and God does not play about the mistreatment of His righteous daughters. God sees your service, and He sees any wrong that has been done towards you. He will repay, and He will make things right. Vengeance is His—your job is to serve.

As feminine wives, we must resist the urge to control our husbands. We are not our husbands, and our husbands are not us. Thus, we can't expect our husbands to respond to things the way we would. As mentioned in previous chapters, we must go with the flow and allow our husbands to be who they are as individuals. Men will naturally resist when they feel trapped and controlled. On the contrary, when men feel respected and honored, they will generally step up and lead their wives and families. As our husbands subject themselves to Christ, we, as feminine wives, subject ourselves to our husbands. This is the biblical order for marriage.

Let me be clear: I am not telling you to be a doormat nor a fool! What I *am* encouraging you to do is embrace your femininity and allow God to use you to be the feminine wife He desires for you to be. I also want to mention here that abuse of any kind is **never** okay! If you are in an abusive situation, I urge you to seek help because abuse is not the will of God.

Some of us may have husbands who are unsaved, and do not have a relationship with Christ. This does not necessarily mean that you need to divorce. 1 Corinthians 7:14 says that "the unbelieving husband is sanctified by the wife." God can use you to reveal Himself to your spouse. Continue to serve your husband and allow God's light to shine through your kind words and actions.

Finally, I encourage every feminine wife to stop complaining. Complaining is not a part of the feminine woman's vernacular, especially the feminine wife. This includes complaining to your friends, family, coworkers, etc. When you are tempted to complain about your husband, choose instead to find a way to make this area of his life easier for him. Men fight many internal and external battles that we are not aware of. We must support our husbands as much as possible when it is within our capacity. Learn how to communicate your needs in a language that he understands, and reach out to a mediator, pastor or counselor to assist you in this area. I want to end this chapter by praying this scripture according to Mark 10:9: "What God has joined together, let not man separate." Amen.

FINAL THOUGHT

Our world would not be what it is today without the feminine woman. Not only are women essential to the preservation of humanity, but women are also essential to the advancement of it. Men and women were meant to coexist, and it isn't good for one to exist without the other. This is clear in Adam and Eve's collaborative relationship in Genesis before the fall of mankind.

The relationship intended for men and women can be seen in the beauty of the waterfall. The role of a man is represented in the rocks. Men are strong and stable, focused, determined, and not easily moved. Rocks provide the immovable structure for water to flow on and between. The role of a woman is represented in the water. Water is free flowing without limitations. Women are meant to flow with creativity and life. It is the strength of masculinity that allows femininity to flow without hindrance.

The feminine woman brings life and creativity to every space she inhabits. Without us, the world would lack vitality and spontaneous adventure. The feminine woman is needed in all areas of society. We provide the nurturing necessary for growth and development. We bring the empathy, innovation, intuition, and flexibility needed to advance in the arts, sciences and even in the highest office in the land.

Walking in freedom and embracing your femininity, therefore, is one of the most important decisions you can make for yourself and your legacy. It is a lifelong process that requires a choice—every decision we make is an opportunity to embrace the power of femininity. Remember to be aware of your environment, emotions, and behavior. Choose to let go of the trauma that's held you captive in the past because, girl, it's time to be free!

Endnotes

Ch 1: What is Femininity: Physical, Mental, & Emotional Components of the Feminine Woman

1. Tim Jewell, "Risk Factors of Having High or Low Estrogen Levels in Males," *Healthline*, Healthline Media, October 22, 2019. https://www.healthline.com/health/estrogen-in-men

2. Adam Taylor, "Why Men and Women Can't Agree on the Perfect Temperature," *The Conversation*, Lancaster University, October 26, 2016. https://theconversation.com/amp/why-men-and-women-cant-agree-on-the-perfect-temperature-66585

3. "Female Reproductive System," *Cleveland Clinic*, Cleveland Clinic Foundation, January 19, 2019. https://my.clevelandclinic.org/health/articles/9118-female-reproductive-system

4. University of New South Wales, "Why Do Women Store Fat Differently From Men?" *Science Daily*, Science Daily, March 4, 2009. https://www.sciencedaily.com/releases/2009/03/090302115755.htm

5. Hai-Jiang Li et al, "Neuroanatomical Difference Between Men and Women in Help-Seeking Coping Strategy," *Scientific Reports* vol. 4 5700, July 16, 2014. https://doi.org/10.1038/srep05700

Ch 2: Blindsided by Trauma: The Disempowered Woman

6.　James Tabery, "Nature vs. Nurture," *Eugenics Archive*, Social Sciences and Humanities Research Council of Canada, April 29, 2014. https://eugenicsarchive.ca/discover/tree/535eed0d7095aa0000000241

Ch 4: Life Through the Lens of a Feminine Woman: Proverbs 31 Study

Finis Jennings Dake, *Dake Annotated Reference Bible* (Lawrenceville, GA: Dake Publishing, 1999), 1107.

About the Author

Daye'Jai Golston was born and raised in the inner city of Cleveland, Ohio where she experienced homelessness, abandonment, drug addiction, and poverty. Despite all the obstacles against her, she was able to overcome each one and create the life of abundance she always dreamt of.

Daye'Jai is the founder and CEO of Daye'Jai Golston Global Enterprises. A gifted motivational speaker, business owner, mother, and coach, Daye'Jai is determined to help others overcome life's challenges and actualize their highest potential. Her life's mission is to help women become who God originally intended for them to be. Daye'Jai believes in the power of service and her desire is to continue using her gifts, resources, knowledge, and skills to change and impact the lives of those around her for the better.

Made in the USA
Middletown, DE
21 September 2024

60854351R00071